AF077253

A *Glimpse* OF *Heaven,*

A *Glimpse* of *Heaven,*

STORIES OF VISIONS & HOPE

By

DARYL J. MINOR

XULON PRESS

Xulon Press
2301 Lucien Way #415
Maitland, FL 32751
407.339.4217
www.xulonpress.com

© 2021 by Daryl J. Minor

A Glimpse of Heaven, Stories of Visions & Hope
Revised

All rights reserved solely by the author. The author guarantees all contents are original and do not infringe upon the legal rights of any other person or work. No part of this book may be reproduced in any form without the permission of the author. The views expressed in this book are not necessarily those of the publisher.

Due to the changing nature of the Internet, if there are any web addresses, links, or URLs included in this manuscript, these may have been altered and may no longer be accessible. The views and opinions shared in this book belong solely to the author and do not necessarily reflect those of the publisher. The publisher therefore disclaims responsibility for the views or opinions expressed within the work.

Unless otherwise indicated, Bible Quotations are taken from the New English Translation (NET Bible). Copyright ©1996-2006 by Biblical Studies Press, L.L.C. Used by permission. All rights reserved.

Contact Information:
Daryl J. Minor
P.O. Box 3396 McAllen, Texas 78502 USA
darylminor@yahoo.com

Paperback ISBN-13: 978-1-6628-1933-9
Ebook ISBN-13: 978-1-6628-1934-6

Dedication

This book "A Glimpse of Heaven Stories of Visions & Hope" is dedicated first of all, to my Lord and Savior Jesus Christ, to our Pastors, Salome and Juanita Villarreal, who have been a pillar of strength and encouragement to my family and I throughout the years, to my wife Marcia Minor, who has been an inspiration to me and the love of my life, to our daughters Marcie Connie Minor, Darcy Ann Minor, and Stacy Ann Perez, who have all brought countless moments of joy, love and happiness into all of our lives, and to my brothers & sisters Dave, Doug, Donna, and Danielle who I admire, greatly respect, and love dearly as well. I would also like to dedicate this diary in memory of my parents John Minor and Mary Minor, my Aunt Sonia Atkinson, my grandmother Agnes Atkinson, my great grandmother Anne Overstreet, my father-in-law Celso Yerena, Sr., my mother-in-law Conchita Yerena, my brother-in-law Ruben Yerena, and my dear friend Kathy Benson, of whom we all love and miss dearly, but by the grace of God we will all see in Heaven again one day.

Table of Contents

Introduction xi
Chapter 1: The Angels Right Hand-Vision 1 1
Chapter 2: The Angel from Heaven-Vision 2 10
Chapter 3: My Mothers Salvation 17
Chapter 4: The Angel's Sang from Heaven-Vision 3 24
Chapter 5: Safely Home-Vision 4 33
Chapter 6: The Women who saw Jesus-Vision 5 42
Chapter 7: Visions of the Rapture-Vision 6 52
Chapter 8: Singing in Heavenly Tongues-Vision 7 59
Chapter 9: Words of Encouragement & Hope 64

Visions of Heaven

"As I observed the angel from Heaven, I first noticed that it had the characteristics of the female gender. I was able to come to this conclusion due to the shape and form of its face, the way in which the hair was colored, and how the hair was positioned on top of its head. I also observed that this angel was around 6 or so feet tall, was very beautiful and slender, had very short blondish colored hair that was parted along the middle, and of which consisted of many different types of small curls that seemed to be perfectly set in place upon the top of its head. Now as I looked upon her face, I noticed that she had ears, a mouth, lips, a nose, eyebrows, eyelashes, and eyes. Her face seemed have some type of indescribable and beautiful coloration or complexion such as occurs with a makeover as well. In regards to the eyes of this angel, she did not have any retinas like we as humans do, but instead they appeared to be very bright like that of pure snow. A great power like lighting seemed to be moving from within her eyes as well. She wore a long pure white gown that was not the same color of white as we know it here on earth, but like a very beautiful pure white that was brighter than a freshly fallen and untouched snow".

Introduction

"To whom much is given, much will be required (Luke 12:48). If you have heard that line of wisdom, you know it means we are held responsible for what we have been given by God. If we have been blessed with talents, wealth, knowledge, time, and the like, it is expected that we benefit others."

In regards to this book A Glimpse of Heaven Stories of Visions & Hope" and as the Bible verse in Luke 12:48 says above, I have been given a gift from God in regards being able to see the visions that are described in this book over the years, and also along with this a great responsibility that pertains to sharing about these visions with as many individuals as I can as well. Because of this, I would like the reader to know that everything that I have shared in this book about the subject of Heaven is a true account based upon what actually happened. They are not fiction, made up fables, or even stories that were written in order to get the attention of others, or with the intent to make financial gain. They are indeed all factual events that really occurred, are based upon warnings, reality as well as truth, are signs that we are indeed living in the last days, and offer further proof that Jesus Christ our Lord is about to return. With that being said, if but one soul is saved from going to hell and goes to Heaven instead as the result of the kind of Eternal Choices one has made, or if even just one life has been touched or even healed for that matter, then my reasons for writing this book will have not been wasted in vain, but instead accomplished, due to my obedience to God, and all for the Glory of God our Creator in the end. God Bless!

The Day of the Lord:

Joel 2:28"And afterward, I will pour out my Spirit on all people. Your sons and daughters will prophesy, your old men will dream dreams, **and your young men will see visions**."

Chapter 1

The Angels Right Hand Vision 1

It was around 1971 when I was only 14 years old, that my Father and Mother finally decided to move from New Haven, Michigan back to Cumberland, Wisconsin. You could say that the experience was rather thrilling, especially since not only would we be moving back to the town where I was born, I would finally be able to see my grandmother Agnes Atkinson, and all of my childhood friends that I grew up with once again as well. I would also be able to spend more time with them after living so far away for so many years. The day finally came that I dreaded, and that was when I would have to go back to school. Oh well, I thought that I could take just about anything, but little did I know just how wrong I would be. There I was, just starting my first year in the 8th grade at Cumberland High School in Cumberland, Wisconsin. To be honest with you, it was rather scary at first, but soon I was able to get used to going to what I thought was a very big place on a daily basis after a very short while. As time went on, I ran into a young man in the 8th grade named Herb Switzer. I did not know it then, but Herb was a born again Christian and the leader of the Morning Prayer group at our high school at that very time itself. He was also the leader of a local Christian youth group in Cumberland, Wisconsin called Youth Alive for Christ or YAC.

Now, not knowing anything about Jesus at the time, I did not understand, nor could I comprehend why Herb was continually being so nice to me, why he kept smiling at me when he would pass by me in the hallways at school on our way to class, or why he kept saying "God Bless you" every time he saw me. However, as time went on, Herb began to ask me when he would see me, if I would like to go to Bible studies with him when I had the chance. In fact, another member of the youth group named Kathy Benson would also ask me the very same thing whenever she saw me as well. At the time however, and because I had a very bad temper and did not understand anything that had to do with God's love, I basically would tell them each time they approached me to just buzz off and to leave me alone from then on. That did not stop Herb or Kathy however, and in fact not only did they both continue to say "God Bless you" to me every time they would pass by me in the hallways at school, they also convinced the other 50 or so members from the Christian youth group Youth Alive for Christ, to also start smiling at me and also ask me if I would like to go to Bible studies with them every single time that they would see me at school as well. By this time, it was finally beginning to annoy me so much that whenever I would see Herb, Kathy, or any of the other members from the youth group at school, I would either run or hide until they were finally all out of sight and nowhere to be found themselves.

Well, let me tell you, Herb and the other youth from the Bible study group continued to be very persistent as time went on. They all kept right on smiling at me, and told me that they never stopped praying for me, nor would they ever give up on me, especially in their efforts they made in regards to trying to talk to me about Jesus during the entire time I spent going through high school itself. It was during the time though that I was in the 11th grade, that I finally started to become very depressed on a regular basis. I realized or thought that I did not have any hope and as the result of all of this, and began to wonder what life was actually all about. I basically spent my whole 11th grade year in high school (1974) crying, starring into the mirror in my bedroom for hours on end at my own refection, listening to rock music that was not very uplifting, while all at that same time trying to figure out a reason just to live. While all of this was taking place in my life, and unbeknownst to me at the time, Herb Switzer, Kathy Benson and the other youth from the YAC Bible study group were still praying for me on a regular basis.

As the months rolled on bringing forth with them another New Year, around 50 or so youth from YAC went to a prayer retreat that was located in Green Lake, Wisconsin during the month of March 1974. It was at this prayer retreat that according to Herb Switzer, all of the youth began to pray for various individuals including myself. When they continued to pray and sing songs of praise and worship to the Lord late into the evening, what appeared to be a white dove flew up out of nowhere in the midst of them and headed through a window in the prayer tower towards the direction of Crystal Lake, Wisconsin where I lived at the time (See Picture The Holy Spirit, March 1974). Now I would like you to know that none of the other youth in the prayer tower, including Herb or Kathy, knew how much their prayers would change my own life or the lives of the many others later on during the fall of that very same year. But in spite of this, they were obedient to the Lord in regards to praying for the souls of others like myself, and did so with great faith knowing that God would hear their prayers. In regards to the very subject of prayer, the Bible says in:

- Proverbs 15:29 that "the Lord hears the prayers of the righteous." In Samuel 22:4-7, David's prayer for deliverance was also heard: "I will call upon the Lord, who is worthy to be praised, so shall I be saved from my enemies. In my distress I called upon the Lord and cried out to my God; "He heard my voice from His temple, and my cry entered his ears." The faithfulness of those young boys and girls in regards to praying for the souls of the lost, including my own, would indeed bring forth many more miracles of salvation and healing later on that year during the fall of 1974 itself.

Now it was during the later part of 1974 around October, that I had not seen Herb, Kathy, or any of the other youth from YAC for quite a while now at school. This was because I was only going to school at that time or for a half a day on a part time basis. Once classes were finished, I would catch a ride so that I could make my way back to my own home each afternoon itself. Although my mother would always be waiting to greet me, I would just go back upstairs to my room once I got home, and in doing so, spend the rest of the afternoon crying while starring at my own reflection in our bedroom mirror. As the days passed by, I would continue to ponder what life was all about, contemplated a reason for living, and wondered if life itself was actually worth living at all. With the coming of November, I finally started to plan in my own foolish way how to go about ending my own life.

As the month of December of 1974 finally approached, I had by that time determined how I would commit suicide, and the actual day and time that this would actually occur. On December 15th, 1974, I took my bottle of aspirin along with a bottle of wine up to my room and lay upon my bed. I rest my head upon my pillow with the intention of finally ending my own life. But by the grace of God, I fell fast asleep at the time and because of this, did not wake up until the following morning of December 16th, 1974 itself. As I arose from my sleep on this day, I was more that determined that this would be the last day I would be alive. Now on this particular day I did not go to school at all, but instead spent most of my time in my room. Although my mother was home she was busy downstairs with housework, and watching her daily soap operas while relaxing in her favorite rocking chair. When the hour finally approached near the time my end would finally come at the doing of my very own hands, I went back downstairs to the living room where my mother was sitting. When I did this, I told her just how much I loved her and that she meant the world to me.

Upon my leaving the living room where my mother was, I remember glancing at the time on the cuckoo clock that hung on the wall just above our kitchen sink, and noticed the time was now 11:45 A.M. in the morning. Once I left the kitchen area, I went straight back upstairs to my bedroom and grabbed my bottles of aspirin and wine with the intent to finally take them as I lay my head upon the pillows on my bed. After crying again with closed eyes for what seemed to be like an eternity, I slowly re-opened my eyes only to gaze upon a brilliant sight beyond description that was positioned right in front of me. The sight I saw was that of a very bright light consisting of the whitish colored right hand of an angel. The palm of the hand was very large, was open, and extended in front of my face about 2 feet in front of me and 3 feet from the floor. As I think back, I recall very clearly that as soon as I saw this beautiful hand, a great peace came over me, I was not longer afraid, time no longer mattered, all sorrow, sadness, and confusion fled from me like the sun's rays of a new day. I was engulfed in what felt like a sea of endless love beyond measure. The hand of this angel was also around three times the size of a human hand, was perfect in every way without flaws of any kind, and had a very pure whitish color that did not exist in any form within our own world as we know it.

As I continued to stare at this angel's hand, I noticed that there was a whitish colored garment of some kind near the portion of the hand that was located near the wrist. Now as I continued to gaze upon the beauty of this angels hand, I recall that it also had lifelines like we do that extended across its palms, all of its fingernails were perfect, and it was proportional in every way, shape, and form. As time went on, the hand began to move in a slow and perfect counter-clockwise motion that was not jittery in nature, and then suddenly came to a stop right in front of me once again. When it did, I could hear a calm voice speaking to me in a love that was not audible in nature, but more like and understanding that penetrated deep within my very heart, mind, and soul. The impression of what I was understanding at the time, was not to be afraid, that everything was going to be okay, that there was indeed hope, that life was worth living, that my life had a purpose, and that Jesus loved me more than I could every know. Being in this place where I was engulfed in an endless sea of love where I did not want to leave and nothing mattered, I saw the angels hand slowly fade away from my sight until it was finally gone. Once this happened, I then got up off my bed, kneeled down next to my bedroom window, and with the room still being filled with so much love and peace, I bowed my head, folded my hands, and then asked Jesus to forgive me of all my sins, to come into my heart, and to be the Lord and Savior of my life because I wanted to live with him forever in heaven. After I did this, I preceded to go back downstairs and when I did, I threw the aspirin and wine bottles away in the trash can, and gazed upon the clock in our kitchen that now said 1:00 P.M. It seemed that only moments before I had gone upstairs to end my life, but because of the prayer of many others, Jesus sent his angel's to fight for my soul, and in doing so, to save my life in the end.

As I proceeded through the kitchen area of our home, I headed towards the living room where my mother was still sitting in her favorite rocking chair. Since she saw me smiling as I approached her, and noticed the glow that was still displayed upon my face due to the change that had just occurred within me, she said "Daryl what happened? You look like you just saw a ghost." I could not tell her at the time about the angel's hand I just saw because for some reason I knew I was not supposed to at the time. Instead, I knew that I need to get a Bible, to go to Church, and start praying for the salvation of others including my own family, just as Herb Switzer, Kathy Benson, and the rest of YAC previously prayed for me. Lastly, although there are no earthly words to describe what I saw, I will try to provide the following example of what the hand of the angel looked like. In doing so, I would like you to understand that even though the color does not exist in this world, nor are the pictures perfect, just try to imagine for a moment the most perfect hand you could ever see, the purest and brightest white you could visualize which is even more white than the color of a fresh Christmas snowfall, and a light brighter than a strike of lightning, and just maybe you will be able to perceive what I saw. In doing so, I hope the picture that I have included will give you some type of an idea as to what I observed during that time itself (See Pictures The Angels Right Hand, and The hand of an Angle-December 16h, 1974).

The Angels Right Hand-vision 1

The Holy Spirit, March 1974

The Angels Right Hand-December 16h, 1974

The Angels Right Hand-vision 1

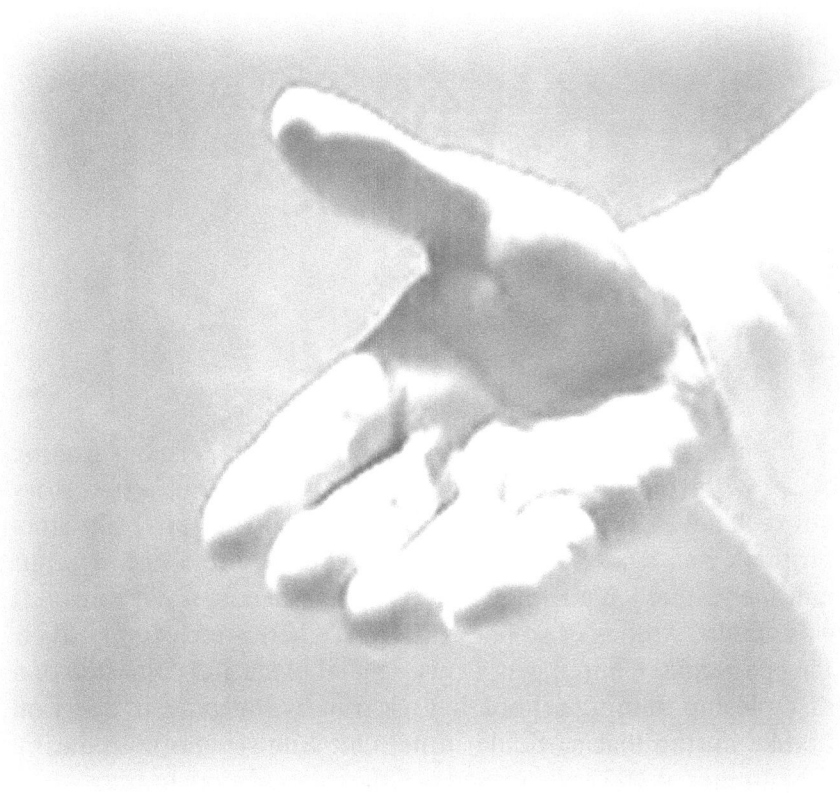

The Hand of an Angle -December 16h, 1974

Chapter 2

The Angel from Heaven - Vision 2

❈

During the year of 1977, I lived in Rice Lake, Wisconsin along with four other Christian brothers of mine in a two story house that was located on 314 Noble Avenue. One of my Christian brothers was named Steve; he and I would go to a non-denominational Church at a Bible school in Weyerhaeuser, Wisconsin. It was about 20 miles or so one way from where we currently lived. This particular Church was a very special place and consisted of a discipleship training school that was run by Pastors Bill and Lou Lemke during that particular time. One Sunday morning during the summer of 1977 we arrived at Church and began to pray while waiting for services to begin. After worshiping the Lord in song and dance, and before the sermon would begin that Pastor Bill Lemke would be giving, we were all asked to sit for awhile in order to enjoy some very beautiful singing from the choir of the Bibles schools student ministry program. I remember very clearly on that day as the choir began to sing, everyone including myself stood up and continued to worship the Lord together. As I was standing, I closed my eyes in deep prayer, and then continued to

The Angel From Heaven-vision 2

sing songs of worship to the Lord along with other members of the Church. Upon opening my eyes, I turned to refocus my attention in the direction where the student choir was standing and singing, and specifically towards the center of the group itself.

It was at this time when I was observing one particular young man who was playing his guitar towards the center of the group while singing a solo that I noticed an angel from Heaven standing right in the middle of the choir towards the center where he was, in a space that was left open, and that was not occupied by any other member of the youth group itself (See Pictures an Angle from Heaven and The Angle from Heaven, Summer1977). As I began to observe this angel from Heaven, I first noticed that it had the characteristics of the female gender. I was able to come to this conclusion due to the shape and form of its face, the way in which the hair was colored, and how the hair was positioned on top of its head. I also observed that this angel was around 6 or so feet tall, was very beautiful and slender, had very short blondish colored hair that was parted along the middle, and of which consisted of many different types of small curls that seemed to be perfectly set in place upon the top of its head. Now as I looked upon her face, I noticed that she had ears, a mouth, lips, a nose, eyebrows, eyelashes, and eyes. Her face seemed have some type of indescribable and beautiful coloration or complexion such as occurs with a makeover as well. In regards to the eyes of this angel, she did not have any retinas like we as humans do, but instead they appeared to be very bright like that of pure snow. A great power like lighting seemed to be moving from within her eyes as well. She wore a long pure white gown that was not the same color of white as we know it here on earth, but like a very beautiful pure white that was brighter than a freshly fallen and untouched snow. The robe that she wore also had some type of gold colored belt attached around the middle portion, and her arms and hands were folded inwards and down in front of her.

As I continued to observe the angel, I noticed that there were two hump like formations protruding outwards from both the left and right side of her back. I also saw what appeared to be wings attached to both the left and right sides of her back that were attached to these humps, of which had feather like formations, and of which seemed to each fold downwards on each side so that they almost touched the ground behind her where she stood. As time went by for what seemed to be about 15 minutes or so, this female angel slowly turned her head towards me and then looked straight at me and directly into my eyes. When she did this, she began to tell me not to be scared, but her mouth was not moving when she said this. She was speaking into my thoughts without talking and yet somehow I was able to understand what she was saying in my own mind. This angel also told me not to tell anyone what I saw until later on in the future, and that I would know when the time came when I should do so. As she continued gazing into my eyes, it was as if two separate beams of light like very powerful spotlights were being projected towards me and through my own eyes themselves.

She was also perfect in every way, without flaw, and was proportional and perfectly balanced as well. In addition, although she appeared to be of the female gender, in regards to her appearance, posture, shape, and form, I now understand from what I observed that there are both female and male angels. This is mainly due to the different types of characteristics that each one displays. Finally after around 15 minutes or so, the angel slowly faded away from my sight. In regards to all of my descriptions of this angel from Heaven, it is very hard to depict or to put into words exactly what I had observed. This is especially true because the different types of colors and characteristics that this angel displayed are nowhere to be found on earth. In order to try to give you an idea however as to what I saw, I have attached pictures of what the female angel I saw more or less looked like. Lastly, I would like to include the following scriptures from the Bible that will help to describe a little more of what I saw, to also give you an idea as to what angels look like, what their eyes look like, and why angels are here. In doing so, I hope you will realize that angels from Heaven are also very much real and do indeed exist as well. The scriptures from the Bible that I speak and that can offer more incite concerning the subject of Angles include the following:

In regards to what Angels look like, the Bible says that they are:

- Matthew 28-24 "His countenance was like lighting and his raiment white as snow",

- Daniel 10:5-6 "Then I lifted up mine eyes, and looked, and behold, a certain man clothed in linen, whose loins were girded with fine gold of Uphaz. His body also was like the beryl, and his face as the appearance of lightning, and his eyes as lamps of fire, and his arms and his feet like the color of polished brass, and the voice of his words of a multitude."

Concerning such things as the personal characteristics of Angels, their roles, abilities, and purpose, the Bible says that they are:

- Vast in number : (Hebrews 12:22; Revelation 5:11),

- They do not die (Luke 20:236),

- They are spirit beings (Hebrews 1:14),

- They are without bodies (Luke 24:39),

- They can assume bodily shape as people (Genesis 19:1-5),

- There is gender among them (Zechariah 5:9-11), and

- They are wise, powerful, have personalities, are moral beings, are superior to people, but vastly inferior to God (2 Samuel 14:20, 2 Peter 2:11, Mark 8:38; 1 Peter 3:22; Hebrews 16). God has also given us angels for the purpose of:

- Protecting-Keeping Gods people out of physical danger, as in the cases of Daniel and the lions, and his three friends in the fiery furnace (Daniel 3 and 6),

- Delivering- Getting God's people out of danger once they're in it. Angels released the apostles from prison in Acts 5 and repeated the process for Peter in Acts 12,

- Strengthening and encouraging- Angels strengthened Jesus after His temptation (Matthew 4:11), encouraged the apostles to keep preaching after releasing them from prison (Acts 5:19-20), and told Paul that everyone on his ship would survive the impending shipwreck (Acts 27:23-25), and

- Caring for believers at the moment of death – In the story of Lazarus and the rich man, we also read that angels carried the spirit of Lazarus to "Abraham's bosom" when he died (Luke 16:22).

As far as the Angel that I saw during this time is concerned, I would like you to view the following pictures that I have included, and although they are not perfect in shape, coloration, and form, I hope that they may give you some sort of idea as to what I observed in regards to the angel from Heaven that I described in this chapter itself.

◈ THE ANGEL FROM HEAVEN-VISION 2 ◈

An Angel from Heaven, Summer 1977

The Angel from Heaven, Summer 1977

CHAPTER 3

My Mothers Salvation

I first started to pray for my mother, father, brothers, sisters, aunts, uncles, and friends back in 1974, when I saw the vision of the angel that I spoke of in chapter one of this book itself. It was at this time that Jesus laid upon my heart to start to lift my family up in prayer on a daily basis and to also believe with all of my heart for their very salvation as well. Now the Bible says that "the effectual fervent prayer of the righteous man availeth much." (James 5:16). Also in Acts 16:13 it says, "Believe on the Lord Jesus, and you and your family will be saved." For the next 13 years of my life, and even as I still do until this day, I still pray for and talk to all of my family members, aunts, uncles, friends, and even compete strangers about Gods plan of salvation that is offered through his son Jesus Christ. In regards to the plan of salvation that I speak of, it is very simple and states that "if you believe in confess with your mouth, Jesus is Lord,' and believe in your heart that God has raised him from the dead, you will be saved" (Romans 10:9, KJV). As I continued to be faithful in my prayers, the Lord spoke to me about Abraham from the Bible.

Abraham had a nephew named Lot, who had a wife and sons, and they all lived in the wicked cities called Sodom and Gomorrah. Now these cities were about to be destroyed for their wickedness, but Abraham (even though he lived far away) prayed to the God of Genesis 18:16-33 in the following prayer:

- Will you indeed sweep away the wickedness with the wicked? Suppose there are fifty righteous within the city, will you sweep away the place and not forgive it for the fifty righteous who are in it? Far be it from you to do such a thing, to slay the righteous with the wicked, so that the righteous fare as the wicked! Far be that from you! Shall not the judge of the earth do what is just? (NJKV).

Now God did indeed hear Abraham's prayer. It was because of Abraham's continued persistence and faith in believing that God would indeed hear his prayer and save Lot and his family in spite of his not knowing when, how, where, or even with whom that made all of the difference. Abraham just prayed a prayer of faith and believed that God would take care of the rest. You could say that God wants us to all be like Abraham, in that we too, are to pray as he did in spite of not even knowing how God will save someone that we too are praying for and of whom we also love.

To provide a financial miracle, to heal a health condition, or for whatever reason, God wants us to be persistent in our prayers. We are to never give up but rather believe by faith, even though we may not see the actual outcomes of our prayers, or the method that God chooses to answer our prayers in his perfect time and place. In this case, through Abraham's prayers of faith, God sent his angels instead of people to provide the way of escape and the way to salvation. In regards to my own family, it was sometime during 1983, that my mother was told that she had acquired stomach cancer. At the time that this happened I was living in Texas, which was well over 2000 miles away. As I talked to my mother on the phone off and on during this year, I spoke to her about the plan of salvation that God himself has provided to us through his Son Jesus Christ our Lord. Now my very first preoccupation was, "How could I possibly save her?" The Lord spoke to me at that time and gave me the answer. He told me to just pray as Abraham did and that he would take care of the rest.

My Mothers Salvation

So as I continued to pray for my mother, especially during the summer of 1987, two very special things happened at that time. The first thing that my mother told me about was what had happened to her during the month of June of that year. This was a weekend camping trip to Cumberland, Wisconsin to a place called Eagles Point. Now as my mother told me, she went down to sit for a while by the shore of the lake and put her feet in the water. As she was doing this, another women from the State of Minnesota, sat right down next to her near the same place where my mother was sitting. She then began to tell my mother that the Lord told her and her husband to come to the same place where my mother was during the same weekend that she was there, and to look for a lady with short blond curly hair sitting next to the lake on the shore. She then did what she was told, found my mother sitting by the shore of the lake, and began to tell her about Jesus and Gods plan of salvation. She then went to talk to her husband, who at that same time, invited my father out to go fishing with him on the lake where my mother already was. As the result of this, the women's husband also began to talk to my father about Gods plan of salvation that was given freely to all those who believe, and that was offered through Jesus his only begotten Son.

In regards to the area of prayer and how God heard my own supplications, you could say that God did indeed here my own prayers after 13 years. He did this by first of all by bringing a complete set of strangers from Minnesota with the intent to plant the seeds of salvation within the very hearts of my mother and father themselves. However, this was only the beginning in regards to the area of answered prayers. The second answer to my prayers occurred during the month of July 1987. It was during this time after visiting with my family in Cameron, Wisconsin, that I was actually planning to finish my Bachelors Degree at the University I was attending in Edinburg, Texas. Before I left however, I was staying at my parent's house during the last days of my stay in Wisconsin before returning back to Texas itself. On this particular day after I woke up, I could feel a great peace overcome me as well as every room within my own parent's house. As the result of this, I walked into the living room where my mother was sitting in her favorite rocking chair, and began to talk to her about many things in life, including Gods plan of salvation.

It was during this time that my mother who was very thin, frail, and weak at the time due to effects of cancer, looked up at my face where she sat with her big blue eyes and said, "Daryl, I would like to live forever with Jesus in Heaven when I die, and would like to ask him to come into my heart." There we were, my mother and I, finally after 13 years of faithful prayer. We finally both knelt down together after all of this time on the living room floor on that bright sunny July day in 1987. As we did, my mother asked Jesus into her heart and to become the Lord and Savior of her life. She did so by repeating the following prayer which states: "Dear God in Heaven, I come to you in the name of Jesus. I acknowledge to you that I am a sinner, I am sorry for my sins and the life that I have lived, I need your forgiveness. I believe that your only begotten Son Jesus Christ shed his precious blood on the cross of Calvary and died for my sins. I am now willing to turn from my sin." You said in your Holy Word, Romans 10:9 "That if thou shalt confess with thy mouth Jesus as Lord, and shalt believe in thine heart that God hath raised him from the dead, thou shalt be saved." Right now I confess Jesus as the Lord of my life. With my whole heart, I believe that God raised Jesus from the dead. This very moment I accept Jesus Christ as my own personal Savior, and according to His Word right now I am saved. Jesus I also thank you for your unlimited grace which has saved me from all of my sins, for dying for me on the cross, and for giving me eternal life. Amen."

It was at this point that my mother looked up at me with tears of extreme happiness running down her face. Full of peace and joy she looked over at me from where she was, and said, "Daryl, my son, I am not scared at all anymore. I feel so much peace inside. I know for sure now that I belong to Jesus now, and because I do, everything is going to finally be okay." We then both got up from the floor where we both had been praying for around an hour or so, and then sat down, talked for awhile longer, and then prayed some more. As time passed, I finally returned back to Texas in order to resume my studies at the University that I had been attending. After a few months had passed, I received a phone call during

October from my father who was with my mother at the Rice Lake Regional Hospital in Rice Lake, Wisconsin. He informed me that my mother was just taken by ambulance from home to the hospital that day since she had been feeling very sick. I then asked to speak to her and then told her once again just how much I loved her and how much Jesus loved her. I also asked her again if she knew where she was going. With her last breaths she said to me "Daryl my son, I just want you to know that I love you very much, and I don't want you to worry because I am at peace now, am no longer afraid or in pain, and that I am going home to be with Jesus."

With my mother headed for Heaven and leaving me behind in this world I was indeed sad, but I was also happy knowing that she would be okay now, that I would once again see her one day, and that she was finally safely home with Jesus. As far as my father, brothers, sisters, aunts, uncles, cousins, friends, and other people are concerned, I continue to pray for them, to talk to them about Jesus, and believe by faith for their salvation. The only thing that I need to do is to just keep on praying like Abraham by faith, and to trust that God will take care of all the rest. Lastly, please see the following pictures and poem that I have dedicated in the loving memory of my mother Mary Ann Minor.

The Plan of Salvation

Home in Heaven Poem

I am home in Heaven, dear ones; Oh, so happy and so bright!
There is perfect joy and beauty
In this everlasting light. All the pain and grief is over,
Every restless tossing passed;
I am now at peace forever,
Safely home in Heaven at last. Did you wonder I so calmly Trod the valley of the shade?
Oh! but Jesus's love illumined
Every dark and fearful glade. And He came Himself to meet me In that way so hard to tread;
And with Jesus's arm to lean on,
Could I have one doubt or dread? Then you must not grieve so sorely,
For I love you dearly still:
Try to look beyond earth's shadows,
Pray to trust our Father's will. There is work still waiting for you, So you must not idly stand;
Do it now, while life remaineth-
You shall rest in Jesus' land. When that work is all completed, He will gently call you Home;
Oh, the rapture of that meeting,
Oh, the joy to see you come!

Chapter 4

The Angel's Sang from Heaven- Vision 3

✾

I met my soon to be wife Marcia during the summer of 1987. I was introduced to her by her sister Connie at the University of Texas Pan American in Edinburg, Texas. It was at this University in a math class that we were taking together, that she began to speak to me about her sister Marcia at the time. She even gave me her phone number, a picture, and the address where she lived, and told me that I should call her as soon as possible as well. Now the day finally arrived when I called her for the very first time on the phone. When I did, I asked her if I could go to her house in order to meet her as well as the rest of her family in person. I remember that after she said yes, I quickly hopped into my car and headed in the direction of her house as fast as I could possibly go. As soon as I realized I was almost there, I suddenly became really nervous and worried if everyone including Marcia would like me when I arrived. Well to my surprise, as I knocked on the front door of the house and soon stepped inside, I was immediately accepted as part of the family by Marcia's father Celso Yerena, and her mother Conchita Garcia de Yerena, the rest of her brothers and sisters, but most of all by Marcia herself. I think that Marcia and her Father Celso especially liked me for the reason being that I was wearing a very long mustache at that time itself.

During the first visit to Marcia's house, her mother asked me to sit at the table for something to eat. As soon as I sat down, I was immediately served a very big glass of freshly made lemonade and some very delicious tacos as well. While I was eating my tacos and drinking the lemonade, I began to choke on the lemonade to the point I was having difficulty breathing during that time itself. As I continued choking, I noticed that Marcia started to cry due to her worrying about my condition. It was then at that very moment that the Lord showed me the beauty of my future wife's heart, and said to me that she would be the one that I would soon marry later on. As the months passed I soon asked Marcia if she would like to be my girlfriend, and later after awhile my fiancé. As we got to know each other better, we would spend more time at Church with her mother and father. We also went to Mexico and other places as well. As far as Marcia's mother and father were concerned, I thought that they were also like she was, very special people, especially due to the close relationship that they all had with the Lord. Most of our time spent together would be talking, joking around, and laughing with a sense of humor at the good things of life. It was not that long after I first met Marcia that I finally asked her to marry me, and it was on February 12th, 1988 that we finally were joined together in holy matrimony at Liberty Temple Church in Pharr, Texas.

Although the day that I got married to my wife Marcia was a very special occasion, her mother could not come to the wedding due to her being very ill at the time. But in spite of this, I thank the Lord that I met Marcia and her family, and for bringing them into my life. Now as time went on, my mother–in-law Conchita, continued to become much worse off with each passing day due to her health condition, and because of this my father-in-law Celso Sr, my wife Marcia, and I finally took her to a hospital that was located in Monterrey N,L., Mexico. It was during one of our visits in June of that year, that I approached the bed inside the hospital where my mother-in-law Conchita lay, and when I did, I could see that she had both of her arms extended up in the air, that she was singing and praying, and that she was looking up towards Heaven at the time. As I came closer to her bed, she calmly and with much love took my hands and looked into my eyes. As she did this, and although she could no longer talk to me at the time due to her worsening health condition, I knew that she was telling me that she loved me, to take care of her daughter Marcia, that she was happy that I married her daughter, that she was happy and at peace, and most of all that very soon she would be going home to be with Jesus. Soon after that, my wife Marcia approached the bed where her mother was, and as she did, her mother lay both of her hands upon her stomach, prayed for her, and then smiled. We did not know it yet, but my wife Marcia was already pregnant with our first daughter Marcie at the time.

As the day went on and after spending time with my mother-in-law Conchita, we all went down stairs for the evening in order to get something to eat, and to find a place to rest for the night. After searching everywhere, we finally found some chairs that were lined up against a wall on a first floor hallway of the hospital. The only thing though, was that these very chairs were all located right next to a very big air vent that also seemed to be connecting to all of the other floors of the hospital itself. In regards to what happened next, I would like you to understand the hospital had a no-noise policy in regards to patients and their visitors, which also prohibited the use of cell phones, computers, and others things like radios, loud noise, and more. The reason being that this was established with the health and well being of the patients in mind themselves. That being the case once my father-in-law Celso Sr., my wife Marcia, and I all sat down on each of our chairs to rest, we soon fell fast asleep for the night. As the evening wore on into the midnight hours and the hustle and bustle of Doctors, Nurses, and patients came to a close, complete silence had now made its way through every hallway and room within the hospital itself. However during the early morning hours of the following day while the sun was still asleep, and before its daylight rays had yet risen, my father-in-law, my wife Marcia, and myself were suddenly woken up to what appeared to be the sound

The Angel's Sang From Heaven-vision 3

of a very large choir echoing down through the air vent next to us, of which was singing songs of praise in unison, in both high and low tones, with both female and male voices, and in a language the none of us had ever heard before within our world as we know it (See Picture–The Angelic Choir from Heaven).

Right after this event occurred, and the noise of the choir had ceased to exist, we all looked around to see where it may have come from, but of which was nowhere to be found. As we continued to search to no avail, we slowly made our way back upstairs to the very room where my mother-in-law was sleeping, and as we did, we approached one of the Nurses in order to inquire as to her health condition at that time itself. Upon doing so, we were unfortunately told that my mother-in-law Conchita had just moment before passed away. The Nurse also told us that at the time of her passing, that she had her hands up in the air extended towards heaven, was singing songs of praise in a language that she did not understand, and that when she passed away, that she also heard what appeared to be a very loud choir singing songs of worship at that very time itself. Once we all were told this, we all realized that the choir we heard downstairs was for real, that it was not made up or in our minds, but that it was an angelic choir that was singing songs of praise as my mother-in-law was welcomed into Heaven to be with Jesus forevermore (See Picture-Welcomed Home by Jesus).

In regards to angelic singing, and to prove that what we all heard does indeed exist, the Bible says:

- Luke 2:12 that "At once the angel was joined by a huge angelic choir singing God's praises.",

- It also says in Luke 2:15: As the angelic choir withdrew into Heaven, the sheep-herders talked it over. "Let's go over to Bethlehem as fast as we can and see for ourselves what God has reveled to us." and in,

- "But as for me, to be able to live is Christ and to be able to die is gain." (Philippians 1:22). Amen!

In regards to the passing away of my mother-in-law Conchita, we were all very sad at first, but at the same time we were also filled with great peace because we all in our hearts and minds that Conchita Garcia de Yerena had now gone home to receive her great reward in Heaven, and to live with Jesus forevermore. Finally, see the following pictures that depict an angelic choir singing, Jesus welcoming my wife's mother Conchita Garcia de Yerena safely home to heaven, and the lyrics to one of my mother-in-laws favorite songs (See Picture-When the Roll is called up Yonder).

The Angel's Sang From Heaven-vision 3

The Angelic Choir from Heaven

A Glimpse of Heaven

Welcomed home by Jesus

◆ THE ANGEL'S SANG FROM HEAVEN-VISION 3 ◆

WHEN THE ROLL IS CALLED UP YONDER

When the trumpet of the Lord shall sound and time shall be no more,
And the morning breaks, eternal, bright and fair;
When the saved of earth shall gather over on the other shore And the roll is called up yonder, I'll be there.

When the roll, is called up yon-der,
When the roll, is called up yon-der,
When the roll, is called up yon-der,
When the roll is called up yonder I'll be there.

On that bright and cloudless morning when the dead in Christ shall rise,
And the glory of His resurrection share;
When His chosen ones shall gather to their home beyond the skies,
And the roll is called up yonder, I'll be there.

When the roll, is called up yon-der,
When the roll, is called up yon-der,
When the roll, is called up yon-der,
When the roll is called up yonder I'll be there.

Let us labor for the Master from the dawn till setting sun,
Let us talk of all His wondrous love and care;

Then when all of life is over, and our work on earth is done, And the roll is called up yonder, I'll be there.

When the roll, is called up yon-der,
When the roll, is called up yon-der,
When the roll, is called up yon-der,
When the roll is called up yonder I'll be there.

Chapter 5

Safely Home Vision 4

My father-in-law Celso Yerena Sr. and I spent many years together and as the result of this, became very close to each other as the years slowly passed by. Although during this time he spoke only in Spanish, and I on the other hand mostly English as well as a little Spanish, we managed to communicate to each other with the help of our Lord, and through the great love that we both had developed for each other in regards to mutual respect itself. As time went on however, it was around the year 1996 that he unfortunately developed congestive heart failure, upon being diagnosed and admitted at a local hospital near where we live. But in spite of this, his medication regimen, the difficulties that he had faced each day in regards to his health condition, and with all of the appointments that he needed to make, he continued to serve the Lord as he always did on a day to day basis itself. He was not a rich man in regards to material wealth by any means, in fact because of his financial situation most of the time he carried little if any money within his own wallet. His riches were held within his heart, and in how he treated the many others that he met.

You see, my father-in-law was the kind of person who bought constant joy into the lives of others wherever he went, weather to a stranger on the street, to the staff at a Doctor's office, to the personnel in the meat market at a grocery store, or even to those who were homeless and begging for food on the street as well. He\ would always greet everyone with a big smile and a positive comment, to bring joy to everyone he met and to brighten there day. During the time he went to Church when he was feeling well, I still can hear his voice to this very day echo the words "Gloria a Dios" (or "Glory to God") in order to proclaim the great love he had for the Lord. Yes, he was the type of person whom you would enjoy being around, and not only would the would the qualities of his own life change one for the better, you would become that much wiser each time you spoke to him or talked to him on any given day. As the years passed by, and his health condition continued to decline, he was admitted back to the hospital once again. This time however, it resulted from a very severe heart attack that he happened on the very day he was admitted back to the hospital itself.

As we all were gathered at the hospital during this time that he was admitted during the Spring of 1995, the Doctors told us that he was not going to make it this time, and even went on to show us medical evidence that showed that he was in a comma and now brain dead. Because of his medical condition at the time, the Doctors at the hospital even asked for permission to remove the oxygen that was being used in order to keep him alive. We decided to hold off on this and thought it would be best to wait to see of his condition improved, so we all prayed that night until the following morning believing at all times for a miracle to take place. The miracle that we had hoped for did indeed come with the dawning of this new day. The miracle came as the Doctors approached us and informed us that my father-in-law Celso Sr. was no longer in a coma, was no longer brain dead, and was very much alive.

Of course, he still had to stay in the hospital for about a week after that in order to recuperate. He needed to regain his strength until he was given the medical clearance he needed to be released and until we were finally able to bring him safely back home. On my father-in-laws arrival to his house he then rested for a few days to re-gain his strength. After he had improved to point of getting around on his own, he told us that he wanted to talk to us in regards to a vision that he had seen during the time that he was in the hospital. As we all gathered around his bed where he was resting on that day, he told us that while he was in the hospital in a coma and considered brain dead, that he saw Jesus come into his room and stand by the end of his bed (See Picture–Jesus our Lord). He then told us that Jesus spoke to him of the many things that where yet to come, and that we were indeed living in the last days before his return. He also told us that it was not time for him to go yet to his new home in heaven, and that God still had some more work for him to do on this earth before he would be called back to his heavenly home. In regards to the visitation that he had with our Lord and Savior Jesus Christ, he went on to say that he was radiant in color, that he was glowing and whiter than snow, and that his eyes were like lightning or beams of very powerful light. He also told us that Jesus was wearing a long, white robe with a golden type belt wrapped around his very waste. He also said that hair was shoulder length, parted in the middle, a little curly on both sides, and appeared to consist of a mixture of brown and light brown colors. His beard was medium in length and he was tall and slender. As soon as Jesus finished speaking to him, Celso Sr. went on to tell us that he then also saw his wife Conchita who passed away 10 years earlier. According to Celso Sr., she was very beautiful, wore a whitish colored type robe, and her face and eyes radiated with an immense type of glowing white coloration, of which reflected a peace and love beyond description (In regards the actual coloration, refer back to what I saw in chapters 1 and 3). In regards to his wife Conchita, she told him that it was not time for him to go to heaven yet, even though he wanted to actually go. She also went on to tell him that he still had some work to do here on earth and that Jesus needed him to take care of it before he called him back home. Well as time went on, my father-in-law Celso Sr. continued to carry out the work that God had instructed him to do, talking to more people about Jesus and the visions that he saw while in the hospital, telling other of his miraculous healing, and also spending more time with family and friends a well.

It was around three years later towards the later part of April 1988 that my father-in-law's health for the second time took at turn for the worse once again. As the result, he wound up back in the hospital again because of another stroke, and upon his release, the Doctors told us that he did not have that much time left to live. However in spite of this bad news, we all continued to spend as much time with him as possible from then on. Now unbeknownst to us, it was during the month of May 1998 that Jesus would be calling my father-in-law Celso Sr. back home.

Now after a few weeks had passed, Mother's Day soon arrived on a Sunday during the same month of May 1998, It was on this particular day, that my-father-in law woke up early that morning and went out to the store to buy his daughter, my wife, Marcia the most beautiful flowers that could be found. As he bought them over to our house later that afternoon on that very same day, he approached my wife, our children, and I, and then proceeded to give all of us very big hugs. After he did this, he went on to tell us just exactly how much he loved us, and said as he always did' ("Dios de Bendiga)", or (God Bless you)" before leaving us all and returning back to his own home. Around 6:00 P.M. that day, my father-in-law called us on the phone and once again told us all just how much he loved us. As soon we got off the phone, we all got ready, and started our way towards evening worship services at Church, but at the same time my wife Marcia felt that something was wrong, and that we should go back to her father's house to see if he was okay.

Upon our arrival at my father-in-laws house I knocked on the front door numerous times, all to no avail. Because of this and due to the situation at hand, I finally took it upon myself to break down the actual door. As I did, my wife Marcia, my daughters, and I, all saw my wife's father lying on his back on the kitchen floor with his hands folded by his side, and with an expression on his face of happiness and peace that I have never seen before. After I noticed and checked his physical symptoms and medical state, I then called the ambulance because by that time I could find no pulse at all. With the sound of the ambulance siren wailing in the distance and on the way to his house, we all kneeled down next to him while holding his hands in great sadness because of our loss. But we were also soon engulfed with a great peace at the same time from the Lord, because we all knew that Jesus came to take him back home. Yes my father-in-law Celso Yerena Sr. lived all of his life for Jesus. He was a faithful servant with all of his heart even to the very end. Because of this, he had gone now to be with Jesus, to see his wife Conchita, and all of the saints in Heaven forevermore.

- "As for me, I am already being poured out as a libation, and the same time of my departure has come. I have fought the good fight, I have finished the race. I have kept the faith. From now on there is reserved for me the crown of righteousness, which the Lord, the righteous judge, will give to me on that day, and not only to me, but to all who have longed for his appearing" {2 Timothy 4:6-8, NRSV).

Finally, please see the following pictures that depict our Lord and Savior Jesus Christ, and our new home in Heaven. Amen!

Jesus our Lord

The Gates of Heaven

Our New Home in Heaven

BEYOND THE SUN

Beyond the sun Even though in this life I lack wealth

I know that at a place called Glory I have
my mansion

A soul lost In poverty

Jesus Christ had mercy On me beyond the sun
Beyond the sun

I have a home, a home A beautiful home

Beyond the sun like this I go walking
Across the world

Many tests surround me And there's temptation too
But Jesus Christ

Who is testing me Will lead me safely

To his mansion beyond the sun Beyond the sun

I have a home, a home A beautiful home

Beyond the sun to each of the races Of human
lineage, Christ

Can grant Complete salvation

And a beautiful house Made by his own hands

has Been prepared at saint Zion, for them
Beyond the sun

Chapter 6

The Women who saw Jesus Vision 5

It was sometime during the summer of 1977 that my other Christian friends Steve, Bruce, Pat, Mike, and I, were getting ready to go to a weekend Christian retreat in Weyerhaeuser, Wisconsin, of which was scheduled to take place on the weekend a few days away. In fact, we were all so excited about the retreat that hardly any one of us could get any sleep at all. As the days drew closer and the time finally came for us to go. We all put our personal items in our bags, jumped in our cars, and then left for what we prayed would be a weekend of blessings without end. As we arrived at the Bible School where the retreat was held, we unpacked our bags, made our way through numerous amounts of other people that were already there, and then checked into the rooms where we all were told to go. Well as the 2 day retreat continued on, we basked in the fellowship with a multitude of other believers, enjoyed the teachings of Pastor Bill Lemke, delicious food, and the other types of activities that had been planned out in advance for everyone to partake in as well.

The Women Who Saw Jesus-vision 5

As the end of the retreat finally came to a close, I was approached by another Christian sister in the Lord right before we all said our goodbyes, and as I was headed for the front door. Now, this sister in the Lord asked me if I had a moment or two to talk with her. The reason being that she had some things she wanted to share with me, and to also ask for prayer for as well. As we began to talk, I began to notice that there were tears in her eyes, and that she had a lot of sadness coming from within inside her too. She told me about her wonderful Christian husband of whom she had been married for 20 years or more, all of the things that they did together, and the plans that they had in store. I was told about her family, that she was born in Mexico, about the 14 year old son she had, and the hope and dreams she had in and what the future would hold. As we talked for an hour or two, she began to cry. She told then that she could not contain her tears or sorrow anymore by that time. The reason being I was told, was that during the previous month her husband went out jogging during the early morning hours near where they lived. Apparently while he was jogging and unbeknownst to her husband at the time, there was a drunk driver on the same road that was not too far behind where he was at the time. As he then turned around and began to head back home, this drunk driver then crossed the median, headed to the other side of the road, and struck him from behind. That day she told me that her husband died, and that she had not only lost her very best friend, but a father for her son, and her partner for life.

At that point we both began to pray, and when we finished I gave her my phone number and told her that if she needed anything, that I was just a phone call away. I also told her about a Christian retreat from Green Lake, Wisconsin where my friends from Youth Alive for Christ went when I was young, and prayed for me at that time well. I mentioned all that happened to me (See Chapter 1 of this book), the angel that I saw, and how the Lord saved me because of this as well. She then thanked me for talking and praying for her, and for telling her about the retreat, and said that she too would try to make plans to go there as well, in the hopes that her miracle would come, and that God would heal her from the sorrow she was also suffering from.

During the months that followed, I talked to this new found sister in the Lord while at Church every once and awhile. After that, I had not seen her for at least 6 months or so since she had not been coming to Church at all. When I did see her, it was during Sunday evening services during the month of June of the following year. After services were over, we all sat down for a bite to eat while there as we always did. But it was during this time that she made an announcement to everyone. She told us that she had something very special to share. As my friends, Pastor Bill Lemke, his wife Lou, and along with 20 or so others including myself, sat around the table waiting with eager expectation to hear what she had to say, she finally approached our table, sat, down, and began to tell us of a special type of miracle she had, and some very good news as well. As she began to share with us about her recent experiences, she began to tell us about the recent events that unfolded before her at the prayer retreat at Green Lake, Wisconsin. As it turns out, I found out at this time that she did take my advice and go to the retreat after all.

It was about a year earlier she said, that the Lord placed upon her heart to take some time off, and in doing so, to go somewhere to meditate and pray so that she could find the peace she needed, and to renew her relationship with the Lord. I doing so, she began to share that she did just that, and while at the retreat in Green Lake, Wisconsin, the first miracle that occurred was the healing of the hurts and sorrow that she held onto for so long, as the result of her late husband's untimely death. The second miracle as she stated did not happen until about 6 months after that, and came in a way that no one else, and not even she would ever expect. You see, she went on to explain, during the last evening of her retreat, she was taking one final walk before saying goodbye. According to her, she was also taking some pictures on her Polaroid camera to keep for memories and as keepsakes at the time. Now in regards to these pictures, apparently it became somewhat cloudy all of the sudden on that bright and sunny day, and as it did, the Lord spoke to her to take a picture towards the clouds in the sky. At the time, this did not make any sense to her and at first she thought it was rather a silly thing to do. But she finally took her old Polaroid camera out and took one last picture and then put the camera and picture away one last time.

As time went on and a few months more passed by, the Lord spoke to her to go look at the picture she had taken of the clouds in the sky. When she did this, it was hard to explain what she saw in regards to what was displayed upon the face of the picture itself. With silence falling upon all of us sitting at the table, she then pulled out the original picture that she had taken with her Polaroid camera that day. As each of us there that night received the picture in our hands, we stared with awe and wonder in regards to what we were all seeing displayed on the face of the picture itself. You see, what we each saw that night on the picture was Jesus our Lord and Savior standing in the clouds. Now as it became my turn to study the picture, you must understand at first that it is impossible to fake a picture of any type on a Polaroid camera itself. That being the case, as I was observing the picture, I saw Jesus standing in the middle of a cluster of surrounding clouds.

From what I as well as the twenty or so others saw that night, he appeared to be tall and slender, his hair was medium in length, parted down the middle, was sort of curly or wavy in nature, and touched his shoulders as well. His beard and mustache were short and protruded downwards about 8 inches or so from his mouth and chin. The robe that he wore consisted of a color like light, was sort of fluffy in certain locations, was whiter and purer than that of snow (See Chapter 1 and 3 in regards to the type of coloration), and the belt that he wore around his chest was made of gold. I could see his nose, mouth, and the parts of his ears that were not covered by his hair. In regards to his eyes though, I could not see any type of retina, but what I did observe to be were areas of pure white light emanating from these very areas themselves. The actual overall formation of his body was solid, yet crystal like, and included a mixture of pure white. As far as his hands were concerned, he was holding also two gold colored leafs attached, and about 6 inches from where the leafs were positioned towards the middle, there was a gold bar attached on the pole that had the words ("INRI") or King of the Jews inscribed in the center of the bar itself. In regards to his hands, I also noticed what looked like to be healed scars on the outer center portions of each one as well. As I continued to look with wonderment at the picture I held in my hand that night, I realized that I was not looking at a fake or doctored photo of some type, and that I was looking at the real thing. I was looking along with others at a picture that was taken of Jesus Christ the King of Kings (Photos taken with the old Polaroid cameras are impossible to fake.)

In regards Biblical descriptions of Jesus are concerned, these would include the following:

- Revelation 1:13-14: "And in the midst of the lamp stands one like a son of man, clothed with a long robe and with a golden sash around his chest. The hairs of his head were white, like white wool, like snow. His eyes were like a flame of fire",

- Daniel 10:5-6: "I lifted up my eyes and looked, and behold, a man clothed in linen, with a belt of fine gold from Uphaz around his waist. His body was like beryl, his face like the appearance of lightning, his eyes like flaming torches, his arms and legs like the gleam of burnished bronze, and the sound of his words like the sound of a multitude",

- Daniel 7:9: "As I looked, thrones were placed, and the Ancient of Days took his seat; his clothing was white as snow, and the hair of his head like pure wool; his throne was fiery flames; its wheels were burning fire," and,

- Matthew 28:3 : "His appearance was like lightning, and his clothing white as snow".

Now as we all returned the photo back to the women that night, she told us that the Lord instructed her just to hold onto it herself from then on. She also went on to talk about the reason that the Lord allowed her to be able to take the photograph as well. Among these were that of hope in regards to knowing that her late husband was with him, the peace she received and the increase in her faith, when she actually saw Jesus for real, as a message that he is separating believers from non believers upon the earth, and that he is coming for his Church. As far as Biblical scriptures that can provide more information as to what was seen in the picture itself, these are as follows:

- Revelation 14:13-20: "And I heard a voice from heaven saying unto me, Write, Blessed are the dead which die in the Lord from henceforth: Yea, saith the Spirit, that they may rest from their labors; and their works do follow them. "And I looked, and behold a white cloud, and upon the cloud one sat like unto the Son of man, having on his head a golden crown, and in his hand a sharp sickle. And another angel came out of the temple, crying with a loud voice to him that sat on the cloud, Thrust in thy sickle, and reap: for the time is come for thee to reap; for the harvest of the earth is time is come for thee to reap; for the harvest of the earth is ripe. And he that sat on the cloud thrust in his sickle on the earth; and the earth was reaped."

No doubt, the parables of Jesus regarding the kingdom of heaven warn us of a separation at His return. The parable of the wheat and weeds tells us the Sower claims His good seed at harvest time, while the tares – the children of the evil one – are gathered by the angels and cast into hell (Matt. 13:26-30, 36-43). Likewise, in the parable of the dragnet, the angels are sent to separate the good fish from the bad fish, which are cast into the blazing furnace (Matt. 13:47-50). "An angel may superintend the execution of the wrath of the judgment of Almighty God, but when the Lord harvests this earth He, Himself, carefully watches over lest one of His least, humblest saints be forgotten or overlooked. There is everything in the Bible to comfort and to give assurance to those who lean on the strong arm of our Lord"

Now, in regards to further examples of what we all saw concerning the picture of Jesus, the staff that he held, and the reason that this women was allowed to see him in the first place, I am including a picture of Jesus that a passenger in airplane took with a

Polaroid camera in 1962 (See Picture–A Picture of Jesus). Now in regards to this particular picture, it does show an outline of Jesus, unlike the picture that we saw of Jesus which was very much real, and crystal clear in every way. As far as the sickle is concerned that Jesus was holding onto with both hands, (See Pictures–The Sickle Jesus was Holding) and (The Sharp Sickle). The sickle that we saw, unlike this sickle, had a blade that was much longer, was curved and sharp, had two knobs for holding onto instead of one, had two golden leafs attached to the top of the sickle, and as said before, had a golden colored bar attached to the middle of the sickle that was engraved with the words ("INRI") which means King of the Jews attached to the pole itself.

In the end, over twenty people including myself were blessed that summer as we all sat down, and heard the testimony from our dear sister in Christ. We were also all touched in more ways than you could ever imagine, because along with this women of God and in addition to her testimony, we too were able to see an actual photograph that was taken of our Lord and Savior Jesus Christ.

THE WOMEN WHO SAW JESUS-VISION 5

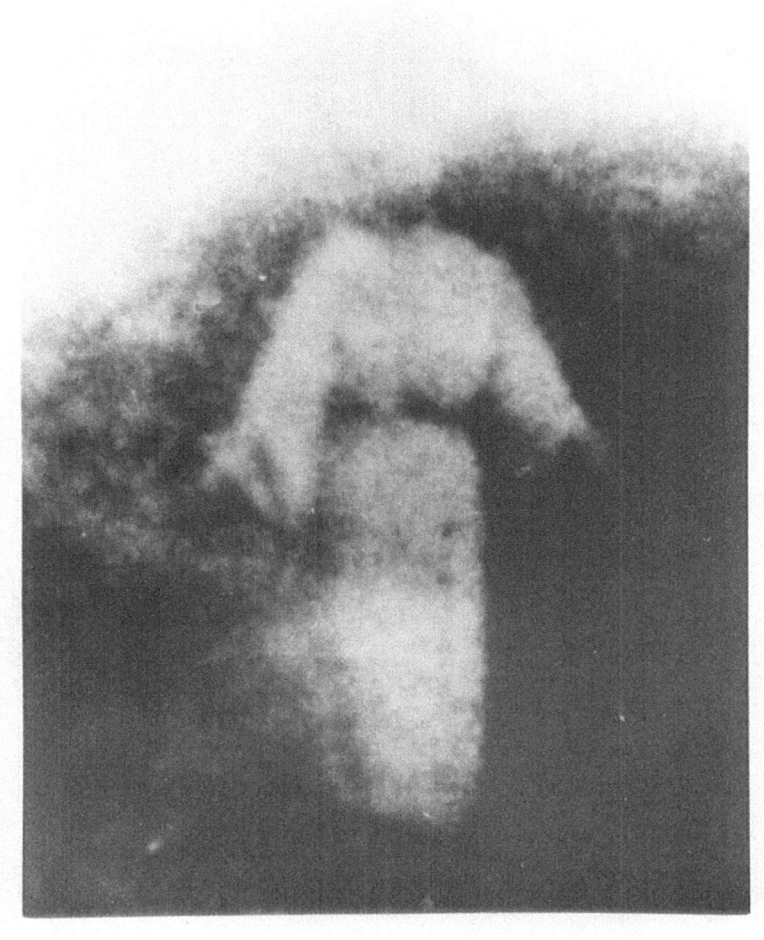

A Picture of Jesus in the Clouds
(This picture was taken with a Polaroid camera during the year1962 through the window of an airplane.) <u>Photos taken with old Polaroid cameras are impossible to fake.</u>

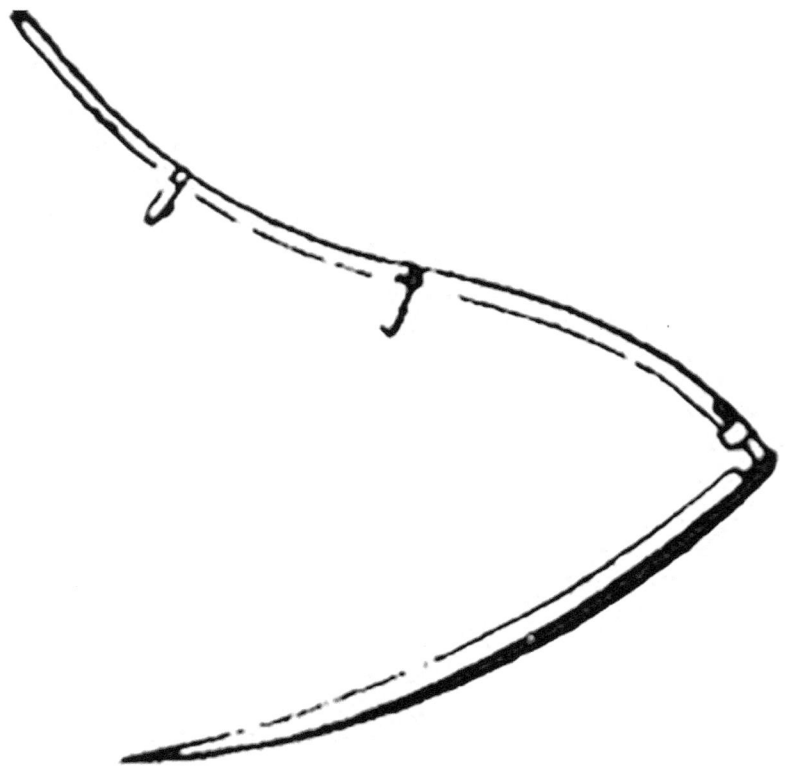

The Sickle like Jesus was Holding

Then I looked, and behold, a white cloud, and sitting on the cloud was one like a son of man, having a golden crown on His head and a sharp sickle in His hand. And another angel came out of the temple, crying out with a loud voice to Him who sat on the cloud, "Put in your sickle and reap, for the hour to reap has come, because the harvest of the earth is ripe." Then He who sat on the cloud swung His sickle over the earth, and the earth was reaped.

Revelation 14:14-16

The Sharp Sickle

Chapter 7

Visions of the Rapture- Vision 6

During the summer of 1978, I was still living in the same house along with the four Christian brothers of mine in the town of Rice Lake, Wisconsin. It was, I believe to be, during the month of June of this year that this particular vision occurred. Now the bedroom where I stayed and called my own was on the second story of our 2 bedroom house, and I had the honor of being able to sleep on the top of a bunk bed within this bedroom itself. In regards to this particular day, I believe that I had a series of visions that concerned the rapture which started around 3:00 A.M. in the following morning. At the time right before these visions or dreams occurred, I began to feel an immense type of peace that swept over me from head to toe, and even though I was still fast asleep physically, it was as if my spirit was wide awake and was observing all that was beginning to take place around me. Now since I was laying on my back with my head facing the ceiling, the first thing that I observed and felt physically, mentally, and spiritually, was the sensation that my whole body was being swept up and lifted off of my bed at a very rapid rate, and by a very powerful force. As this was taking place, this first thing that I saw was my face and body approaching the upper portion of our bedroom ceiling. As this was going on I remember looking back down where I had been previously and realized that my physical body was no longer there even though my blankets, pillows, and pajamas still were.

As I continued to move ever closer towards the ceiling in my bedroom at a very rapid rate, I remember turning my head back downwards once again just to see the windows and walls in my bedroom, along with the desks, chairs, clothes, bed, and pictures on the walls and night stand quickly pass by underneath me. Once I had approached the top of our bedroom ceiling to the point I was about to go through it my body quickly flew back down, and I found myself lying flat on my bed looking upwards at the ceiling once again. In regards to what I had just happened, I realized that although my body may have been asleep at the time my soul was very much awake, I knew that what I had just experienced was very much real, was not a dream, and as the result, I was totally aware of everything that was going on around me. I also believe that what I saw and felt was a warning for both myself and others in regards to what will occur when Jesus returns for his Church.

In regards to a scriptural explanation of what the rapture is, the Bible explains more about this in the following scriptures:

- Listen, I tell you a mystery: We will not all sleep, but we will all be changed-in a flash, in the twinkling of an eye, at the last trumpet. "For the trumpet will sound, the dead will be raised imperishable, and we will be changed. For the perishable must clothe itself with the imperishable, and the mortal with immortality" (1 Corinthians 15:51-53).

Other scriptures that explain more about the rapture include 1 Thessalonians 4:13-17: "Brothers, we do not want you to be ignorant about those who fall asleep, or to grieve like the rest of men, who have no hope. We believe that Jesus died and rose again and so we believe that God will bring with Jesus those who have fallen asleep in him. According to the Lords own word, we tell you that we who are still alive, who are left till the coming of the Lord, will certainly not precede those who have fallen asleep. For the Lord himself will come down from Heaven, with a loud command, with the voice of an archangel, and with the trumpet call of God, and the dead in Christ will rise first. After that, we who are alive and are left will be caught up together with them in the clouds to meet the Lord in the air. And so we will be with the Lord forever."

Now I believe that the vision I saw was very much real, and that I was allowed to experience as well as see this since Jesus is coming back very soon for his Church. For this reason, not only did he want me to be prepared because of this, I also believe that the Lord wanted me to tell others that he is also coming very soon so that they can be prepared as well. In regards to Jesus return for his Church, this can be seen in regards to scriptures that point to us living in the last days. Some of these scriptures include the following:

- Luke17:22-37: "The days will come when you will long to see one of the days of the Son of Man, and you will not see it. They will say to you, "Look there!" do not go away, and do not run after them. For just like lightning, when it flashes out of one part of the sky, it shines to the other part of the sky, so will the Son of Man be in His day. But first he must suffer many things and be rejected by this generation. And just as it happened in the days of Noah, so shall it be also in the days of the Son of Man: they were eating, they were drinking, they were marrying, they were being given in marriage, until the day that Noah entered the ark, and the flood came and destroyed them all.",

- It was the same as happened in the days of Lot: they were eating, they were drinking, and they buying, they were selling, they were planting, and they were building; but on the day that Lot went out from Sodom it rained fire and brimstone from Heaven and destroyed them all. It will also be just the same on the day that the Son of Man is reveled. On that day, the one who is on the housetop and whose goods are in the house must not go down to take them out; and likewise the one who is in the field must not turn back. Remember Lot's wife. Whoever seeks to keep his life will lose it, and whoever loses his life will preserve it. I tell you, on that night there will be two in bed; one will be taken and the other will be left, and in

- There will be two women grinding at the same place; one will be taken and the other will be left. Two men will be in the field; one will be taken and the other will be left. And answering they said unto Him, "Where Lord?" And he said unto them, "Where the body is, there also the vultures will be gathered."

As far as other prophetic scriptures from the Bible that also point to the fact that Jesus is indeed coming very soon for his Church, these can be seen in the following verses as well:

- Matthew 24:6, NKJV. "You will hear of wars and rumors of wars, but see to it that you are not alarmed. Such things must happen, but the end is still to come.",

- Matthew 24:7-8, NKJV. "There will be famines and earthquakes in various places. All these are the beginning of birth pains.",

- John 2:18, NKJV. "Little children, it is the last hour; and as you have heard that the Antichrist is coming, even now many antichrists have come, by which we know that it is the last hour",

- II Timothy 3:1-5, NIV. "But mark this: There will be terrible times in the last days. People will be lovers of themselves, lovers of money, boastful, proud, abusive, disobedient to their parents, ungrateful, unholy, without love, unforgiving, slanderous, without self-control, brutal, not lovers of the good, treacherous, rash, conceited, lovers of pleasure rather than lovers of God—having a form of godliness but denying its power. Have nothing to do with them.",

- Luke 21:25-26, NIV. "There will be signs in the sun, moon, and stars. On the earth, nations will be in anguish and perplexity at the roaring and tossing of the sea. Men will faint from terror, apprehensive of what is coming on the world, for the heavenly bodies will be shaken.",

- I Thessalonians 5:2-3, NIV. "For you know very well that the day of the Lord will come like a thief in the night. While people are saying, 'Peace and safety,' destruction will come on them suddenly, as labor pains on a pregnant woman, and they will not escape.",

- Matthew 24:14, NIV. "And this gospel of the kingdom will be preached in the whole world as a testimony to all nations, and then the end will come.",

- Matthew 24:42-44, "So be prepared, for you don't know what day your Lord is coming. Just as a man can prevent trouble from thieves by keeping watch for them, so you can avoid trouble by always being ready for My unannounced return." and in,

- Luke 21: 28, NKJV. "Now when these things begin to happen, look up and lift up your heads, because your redemption draws near."

Finally, I would like to share with you the following pictures, of which are just some of the many examples of what the rapture may actually look like when it finally takes place. I will see you here, there, or with Jesus in the air. Amen

The Rapture of the Church

The Dead shall rise First

CHAPTER 8

Singing in Heavenly Tongues Vision 7

Now it was around September or October of 1978. During this time I was still living in Rice Lake, Wisconsin with five Christian brothers of mine in the two story house that I had already been living in for a few years thus far. In regards to this particular experience that I had, it occurred around 2:00 A.M. in the morning. At the time, my bedroom was still located at the top of the same bunk bed that I had been occupying for quite some time now. As I look back on this experience and what took place, I often think about what Heaven will be like and the types of sounds that we will all hear one day as we all sing praise to our Lord and Savior Jesus Christ. As far as the beautiful and indescribable experience that I would soon be blessed with, it occurred during the early morning hours on a Sunday, which was on the same day that we would all soon be going to Church. The night before this event happened, I recall getting ready for bed and then climbing up to the top of the bunk bed where I was to sleep for the night. As soon as I lay down in my bed I leaned forwards to say goodnight to my dear friend Pat Davis who lay on the bottom bunk below me. Once I did this, I then proceeded to say my regular evening prayer, laid down upon my bed upon my back with the rest of my body as well as my head facing upward towards the ceiling, and then began to drift off into slumber land for what I prayed would be a good night's sleep. As time itself continued to past by with the ticking on the clock, I recall suddenly and very peacefully waking up from my sleep, and as I did, then hearing the sounds of angelic singing coming from somewhere in the room. It was a sound of which I had never heard before with my ears in any type of shape or form, and did not exist on our world as we know it. This angelic sound that I heard consisted of a combination of different types of pitches and levels that seemed to be blended in a perfect and harmonious unison with one another from high, low, and medium tones, and also sounded like someone speaking in Latin.

As I began to focus more as to the location of this beautiful sound that I was hearing, I finally crossed my eyes and looked down toward my own mouth and discovered that this was the source where these sounds and singing had emerged. I was not scared at all upon my discovery, but was rather peaceful at the time. Now as I continued to observe as well as listen to what my own mouth was doing at the time, I realized that I was not controlling in any way the movement of my mouth, or my vocal cords that had been the source and cause of what I had been hearing. The sounds I heard were perfect in nature, consisted of very fast paced high and low pitched tones, of which were without flaw, and like something one would hear in an opera. As my mouth kept singing in these beautiful melodies that seemed to come from Heaven, I continued to watch and listen to all that was going on, until I regained control of my vocal cords and mouth, and the singing slowly came to a stop. Once this happened, I looked back down under my bed to see if the singing had awakened my friend Pat who lay below me on his own bed. But to my surprise I found that he had not been disturbed in any way, but was still snoring and in a deep peaceful sleep. In regards to what I had experienced this day, the Bible teaches us that this is called speaking in tongues. In regards to speaking in tongues:

- Paul said, "John's baptism was a baptism of repentance. He told the people to believe in the one coming after him, in Jesus.' On hearing this, they were baptized into the name of the Lord Jesus. When Paul placed his hands upon them, the Holy Spirit came on them, and they spoke in tongues and prophesied (Acts 19:4-6), and

- "They saw what seemed to be tongues of fire that separated and came to rest on each of them. All of them were also filled with the Holy Spirit and began to speak in other tongues as the Spirit and enabled them" (Acts 2:3-4). In this case though, my spirit was actually singing in tongues to God through my mouth while I was asleep singing praises and supplications unto his glorious name. As far as what was being said, I do not know, but the Bible teaches that "the Spirit, itself maketh intercession for us with groanings which cannot uttered" (Romans 8:26, KJV).

Lastly, does this mean that one will not go to Heaven, is not a Christian, or does not have Jesus in their hearts if they cannot speak in tongues? Of course not, for every Christian or true believer has already received the Holy Spirit once they asked Jesus into their hearts and can still go to heaven without having to speak in tongues. The gift of tongues is a gift that all Christians can freely receive just by asking. The Bible also says the following:

- Now to each one the manifestation of the Spirit s given for the common good. To one there is given through the Spirit the message of wisdom, to another the message of knowledge by means of the same Spirit, to another faith by the same Spirit, to another the gift of healing by that one Spirit, to another miraculous powers, to another prophecy, to another distinguishing between spirits, to another speaking in different kinds of tongues, and to still another, the interpretation of tongues. All these are the work of one and the same Sprit, and he gives them to each one, just as he determines (1 Corinthians 12:7-11).

In the end, Jesus has given to all those who call upon his name many different types of spiritual gifts through the Holy Spirit. All a Christian needs to do is ask and continue to always believe in regards to the types of gifts that the Lord has for them. If they do so, he will take care of everything else in his perfect time and place. As far as the Holy Spirit is concerned, I have included some pictures that the Bible uses to depict or represent it. In doing so, hopefully you will be able to have an even greater idea as to the power and beauty of the Holy Spirit itself.

GIFTS OF THE HOLY SPIRIT

WISDOM
To value the things of God

UNDERSTANDING
To grasp faith's mysteries

COUNSEL
To make wise decisions

FORTITUDE
To strengthen your will

KNOWLEDGE
To enlighten your mind

PIETY
To love and serve God

FEAR OF THE LORD
To respect God's majesty

The Power of the Holy Spirit

Chapter 9

Words of Encouragement & Hope

Finally the hope that we all have in the end then, is a reality and not a feeling, carries no doubt, is a sure foundation upon which we base our lives, and is believing that God always keeps His promises (See Picture Our only Hope). It is also knowing that no matter how dire the circumstances a person is faced with during one's own life, that there is always hope, that there is indeed a light at the end of every tunnel, that prayer is very much real, that miracles do indeed happen every single day, and that Jesus will always be there to help and heal all of those who call upon his precious and wonderful name. The most important of hopes that we all may have however, is that of eternal life of which Jesus has given freely to all to receive. This can be seen in the following scriptures:

The Bible says there is only one way to Heaven:

- Jesus said: "I am the way, the truth, and the life: no man cometh unto the Father but by me." (John 14:6, NIV) **Good works cannot save you.**"For by grace are ye saved through faith; and that not of yourselves: it is the gift of God: Not of works, lest any man should boast." (Ephesians 2:8-9, NIV).

Trust Jesus Christ today! Here's what you must do:

- **Admit you are a sinner.** "For all have sinned, and come short of the glory of God" (Romans 3:23, NIV)."Wherefore, as by one man sin entered into the world, and death by sin; and so death passed upon all men, for that all have sinned" (Romans 5:12, NIV). "If we say that we have not sinned, we make him a liar, and his word is not in us" (1 John 1:10, NIV).

- **Be willing to turn from sin (repent).** Jesus said: "I tell you, Nay: but, except ye repent, ye shall all likewise perish" (Luke 13:5, NIV). "And the times of this ignorance God winked at; but now commandeth all men everywhere to repent" (Acts 17:30, NIV).

- **Believe that Jesus Christ died for you, was buried, and rose from the dead.** "For God so loved the world, that he gave his only begotten Son, that whosoever believeth in him should not perish, but have everlasting life" (John 3:16, NIV). "But God commendeth his love toward us, in that, while we were yet sinners, Christ died for us" (Romans 5:8, NIV)."That if thou shalt confess with thy mouth the Lord Jesus, and shalt believe in thine heart that God hath raised him from the dead, thou shalt be saved." (Romans 10:9, NIV).

- **Through prayer, invite Jesus into your life to become your personal Savior.** "For with the heart man believeth unto righteousness; and with the mouth confession is made unto salvation" (Romans 10:10, NIV). "For whosoever shall call upon the name of the Lord shall be saved" (Romans 10:13, NIV).

What to pray: Dear God, I am a sinner and need forgiveness. I believe that Jesus Christ shed His **precious blood** and died for my sin. I am willing to turn from sin. I now invite Christ to come into my heart and life as my personal Savior.

"But as many as received him, to them gave he the power to become sons of God, even to them that believe on his name" (John 1:12, NIV). "Therefore if any man be in Christ, he is a new creature: old things are passed away; behold, all things are become new" (2 Corinthians 5:17, NIV).

If you have received Jesus Christ as your Savior, as a Christian you should:

- **Read your Bible every day to get to know Christ better.** "Study to show thyself approved unto God, a workman that needeth not to be ashamed, rightly dividing the word of truth" (2 Timothy 2:15, NIV). Thy word is a lamp unto my feet, and a light unto my path" (Psalm 119:105, NIV).

- **Talk to God in prayer every day.** "And all things, whatsoever ye shall ask in prayer, believing, ye shall receive" (Matthew 21:22, NIV). "Be careful for nothing; but in everything by prayer and supplication with thanksgiving let your requests be made known unto God" (Philippians 4:6, NIV).

- **Be baptized, worship, fellowship and serve with other Christians in a Church where Christ is preached and the Bible is the final authority.** "Go ye therefore, and teach all nations, baptizing them in the name of the Father, and of the Son, and of the Holy Ghost" (Matthew 28:19, NIV). "Not forsaking the assembling of ourselves together, as the manner of some is; but exhorting one another: and so much the more, as ye see the day approaching" (Hebrews 10:25, NIV). "All scripture is given by inspiration of God, and is profitable for doctrine, for reproof, for correction, for instruction in righteousness" (2 Timothy 3:16, NIV).

- **Tell others about Christ.** "And he said unto them, Go ye into all the world, and preach the gospel to every creature" (Mark 16:15, NIV). "For though I preach the gospel, I have nothing to glory of: for necessity is laid upon me; yea, woe unto me, if I preach not the gospel!" (1 Corinthians 9:16, NIV). "For I am not ashamed of the gospel of Christ: for it is the power of God unto salvation to everyone that believeth; to the Jew first, and also to the Greek" (Romans 1:16, NIV).

When all is said and done then, and when one asks Jesus into their hearts, they do indeed have great hope for every tomorrow, will never be alone or forsaken even during the darkest of hours or deepest of valleys, will always be protected, carried, and guided in whatever circumstance they may find themselves to be, and finally at the end of life's journey, will be escorted into Heaven to an eternity of endless joy that awaits them one day when they finally pass away (See Picture- No Greater Love).

In closing then, I pray that you were blessed as well as touched in a special way by this book, that it has strengthened your faith, given you strength to believe and go on, and either saved you or brought you closer to Jesus our Lord and Savior. I also hope and pray that you, too, have or will become fishers of men's souls for Jesus just like me. If this is the case, then I will know that my purpose for writing this book has not been in vain and that Jesus has indeed been glorified in the creation and publication of it as well.

Lastly, before you go, please view the following Bible scriptures as well as pictures, which I pray will not only be a blessing to you, but also encourage you as much as they have encouraged me:

All of life is here summed up in one verse.

- "While I am here on his earth," the Psalmist prays to the Lord, "You will *guide me*. You will give me the direction I need for each step of the way. You will never leave me or forsake me. You will help me when I stumble and you will steer me when I lose my way. What's more, you will guide me *with thy counsel*. This is no mere human, fallible leader. You are an all-knowing, all-wise escort. You will never give me wrong advice or send me in a wrong direction. I will never meet a problem for which you do not know the solution and will never get so off course that you cannot guide me back to safety. However, that is all just life on earth! Afterward, you will *receive me to glory*. After you have carefully and lovingly directed my way here, you will usher me into your glorious presence in heaven. There is no intermediary state – death is not a tunnel, it is a door. When you release my hand in this world, you will receive me into the next. There is no "sending"; there is only *guiding* and then *receiving* – no time apart from you. Death, where is your sting? Grave, where is your victory? Devil, where is your terror? "My God will guide me with His counsel and then receive me to His glory, Psalms 73:24".

Our Only Hope

A Glimpse of Heaven

No Greater Love

Never Alone

About the Author

Daryl J. Minor currently lives at home with his wife and two daughters in McAllen, Texas. He is retired from the military and has worked in the social work and education sectors for over 30 years. He holds also a Bachelor's Degree, two Master's Degrees, and numerous other titles as well. Daryl and his family are also current and active members of Liberty Temple Pentecostal Church in Pharr, Texas, where they continue to attend and have done so faithfully for more than 28 years.

Daryl J. and Marcia G. Minor

Some Final Words

This book "A Glimpse of Heaven, Stories of Visions & Hope" is about many of the true to life and factual experiences that other individuals and I have had since 1974, in regards to visions, stories of hope, and most of all, about God's precious gift of eternal life that we can all have through his one and only son Jesus Christ our Lord. It is my hope that after reading this book, and the many passages of scripture from the Bible that are written within it, that you will come to understand that we are indeed living in the last days right before Jesus returns for his Church, that Heaven and Hell are not some fictionist or made up place but rather are very real, that Jesus, the Holy Spirit, Angel's, Demon's, and the Devil do also exist and are very much real, and that man does indeed have a soul that will feel, think, and live forever once a person's body ceases to exist in this temporal world of ours as we know it. I also pray, that your life will be touched, and that you will come to understand that in spite of all we go through on our pilgrimage through this Earth, that Jesus will always be there to help as well as save all of those who call upon his precious and wonderful name.

The Day of the Lord

And afterward, I will pour out my Spirit on all people. Your sons and daughters will prophesy, your old men will dream dreams, **your young men shall see visions**. Even on my servants, both men and women, I will pour out my Spirit in those days. I will show wonders in heavens and on earth, blood, fire, and billows of smoke. The sun will be turned to darkness and the moon to blood before the coming of the great and dreadful day of the Lord. And everyone who calls on the name of the Lord will be saved. For on Mount Zion and in Jerusalem there will be deliverance, as the Lord has said, among the survivors whom the Lord calls (Joel 2:28-32).

Mount Zion

More books from the Author:

Through the Valley,
A Dairy of Hope,
The Road to Nowhere,
A Story of Forgiveness & Hope,
Hell is Real,
A Dairy of Visions & Hope

Available for Sale on Xulon Press.com, Amazon.com, and Barnes & Noble in Paperback, E-Book, and in the Audio Versions on Amazon.com, Audible, iTunes, and Xulon Press.com as well.

www.ingramcontent.com/pod-product-compliance
Ingram Content Group UK Ltd.
Pitfield, Milton Keynes, MK11 3LW, UK
UKHW041955230426
12048UKWH00008B/345